"I've known Joe for 3 years now and I must admit it's rare to meet a strength coach whose as good as Joe is when it comes to training baseball players. The results he gets his baseball players in strength and conditioning speak for themselves, but the real results lie in the impact he has on all of his athlete's mindsets."

-Paul Reddick
Director of Yogi Berra Museum

"In order for an athlete to reach their on-field potential they should maximize their physical potential. Joe has worked with countless of my players and in each instance Joe's work and tutelage has improved their performance, enjoyment of their game, overall athleticism and most importantly their confidence. I've seen firsthand how much my players have dramatically improved their strength, mobility, nutrition, and recovery ability while also being more resilient to injuries. I whole heartedly recommend Coach Joe and his programs."

-Bryan Henton
Baseball Instructor

"To the best trainer in the world, thank you for making me a complete player."

-John Rodriguez
2006 World Series Champ St. Luis Cardinals

The PARENTS GUIDE TO STRENGTH TRAINING FOR BASEBALL

The PARENTS GUIDE TO STRENGTH TRAINING FOR BASEBALL

"One of my goals for the off season is to get strong & have as much endurance as possible and I plan on accomplishing them by working hard"
— Adrian Gonzalez

Let's face it, choosing the right strength and conditioning program for your son is no easy task. There's so much bad information out there from seemingly credible sources: how to throw harder, how to run faster, or when is the right time to start strength training?   All of this information can be confusing and frustrating for parents.

I know this because not only am I the owner of GameChanger Strength & Performance in Union County, N.J., I am also a former college baseball player and I've come up through this same confusing system.   I know how challenging and frustrating my "growing up" in baseball was for my own parents. For the past five years, I've helped over 1,000 baseball players throw harder, run faster, hit the ball with more power, and perform to the best of their ability.

Throughout this book my goal is to provide you, the reader, with the educational resources needed to make an informed decision when you decide to get your son involved in a strength and conditioning program. In just a moment, I'll share with you my knowledge and insight about strength training for baseball. We'll cover everything you need to know including increasing velocity, preventing injuries, speed and agility training, common baseball training myths, and much more.

Plus, at the end, I'll offer four recommendations that will help you make an informed decision when choosing a strength and conditioning coach, and I'll give you five questions you should ask a strength and conditioning coach before you sign your son up for his program.

Are you interested in training at GameChanger?
Call us directly at (908) 376-9002 to get
your free, no obligation, assessment for your son.

Or email me at Joe@GameChangerGym.com
for more information on how
we can help your son.

Chapter 1: Strength Training For Baseball

"Strength training is key to building my endurance on the mound" - Justin Verlander

Growing up as a baseball player, I was always told by my coaches that strength training was dangerous because it would make me tight and bulky. After all of my years of playing baseball - and now helping over 1,000 baseball players throw harder, run faster and be more explosive - I can assure you that there is no truth behind that statement.

Strength training is critical for all baseball players, because it's the foundation upon which all other physical attributes are built. If you want to get faster, more explosive, more agile, improve your flexibly and mobility, or increase your stamina and endurance - it all starts with building a solid foundation of functional baseball strength. Most importantly, proper strength training will help to bullet proof your body from injuries.

Baseball players are unique athletes and have different needs than football players, basketball players, and other sport athletes. For example, did you know that pitching is the fastest motion in all sports? The arm internally rotates at more than 7,000 degrees per second, so it goes without saying that you need to be cautious about how you manage the shoulder.

Baseball is also a sport where you do everything with just one side of your body. You either throw righty or lefty, bat righty or lefty, you always run the bases in the same direction, and so on. Over time this one-sidedness will lead to imbalances throughout the body and must be accounted for in your training.

Another unique aspect of baseball, when compared to other sports, is rotational power. The athlete's ability to produce rotational power directly impacts hitting power and throwing velocity.

There is also a lateral component to the game of baseball that must to be accounted for in training. Whether pitching, running the bases, or fielding, the athlete needs to be quick and explosive, moving side to side. Whether you're fielding a ground ball in the hole, tracking down a fly ball in the outfield, or running the bases, you must be explosive, moving side to side. In the next chapter you'll discover exactly how to increase bat speed and velocity with proper strength training.

Are you interested in training at GameChanger?
Call us directly at (908) 376-9002 to get
your free, no obligation, assessment for your son.

Or email me at Joe@GameChangerGym.com
for more information on how
we can help your son.

Chapter 2: How To Increase Bat Speed

"Baseball can be slow in many ways. The action starts with when the pitcher delivers the ball. But the action really starts when the crack of the bat happens."
– Call Ripken Jr.

Bat speed is critical to success as a baseball player. Increasing bat speed allows the athlete to see the ball longer and catch the ball deeper in the zone. This extra time translates into better contact and better identifying balls and strikes. Instead of guessing what pitch is coming, the hitter is able to adjust to curveballs or changeups and still able to react to the fastball.

Increased bat speed also means hitting the ball with more power. With more power, bloop singles will turn into line drives in the gap, groundballs in the hole will turn into base hits, singles will turn into doubles, doubles into triples, and triples into homeruns. In a nutshell, increased bat speed will make for a better and more complete hitter.

Many coaches think that bat speed can't be improved through proper strength training. These coaches are flat out wrong. How many times have you heard a coach tell your son to make an adjustment in stride, load, hand positioning or anything related to the swing, but no matter how hard your son tried he just couldn't do it. This happens quite often and the reason why isn't because he's not listening or not trying, but because he physically can't make the mechanical adjustments he needs to because he doesn't have the mobility and stability to be in the proper positions in which his coach wants him.

This is where proper strength training comes into play. Proper strength training will increase your athleticism, which will allow you to make adjustments and get into better mechanical positions. Don't believe a coach that tells you that you can't increase your bat speed with proper strength training.

Below, you'll learn the 3-step system we use at GameChanger Strength & Performance to help our baseball players increase their bat speed and you'll also discover the best exercises to improve bat speed and hitting power.

Step 1: Build A Strong And Functional Lower Body

If you want to start hitting the ball with more power and increase your bat speed, you have to focus on building a solid foundation of lower body strength. The lower body is what produces the power when you swing a bat, so you need to have a functionally strong lower body.

Having a functionally weak lower body is like trying to build a house on sand. Think about this analogy - your lower body is like an engine of a car - the bigger and stronger the engine, the more powerful the car will be. Without this foundation of strength, you will not be able to produce much more power.

Step 2: Build A Strong And Stable Core

Chances are you've heard the core is important for baseball training, but do you really understand why it's so important? In order for you to understand, I'll break it down step-by-step for you. Imagine being in your batting stance, as you get ready to take your swing, your legs produce the power. In order for that power to get projected onto the baseball, it has to be transmitted through your core to your upper body and onto the baseball. Simply put, a strong and stable core will help you effectively transfer power generated from your lower body to the upper body and onto the baseball. If you have a weak core, you're going to leak out energy and power. In other words, you are not going to use all the power you have because you are only as strong as your weakest link.

You could have really strong legs but if you have a weak core you're not going to effectively transfer all of that power. You won't hit the ball as hard as you can. Increasing core stability is critical for baseball players. Let's go back to our car analogy. If you have a car that has 1,000 horsepower but a weak drivetrain that transmits that power to the wheels and the tires, the car won't be able to use all the horsepower it's capable of generating.

Step 3: Increase Rotational Power

In Steps 1 and 2 we are setting the foundation. Once we have a strong lower body and core, we focus on building rotational power. The best way to build rotational power is through rotational medicine ball throws. Before we dig deeper into this, you should know that way too often I see baseball players skipping the first two steps: building a strong lower body and core.

Instead they go right to Step 3 and try to implement rotational throws. This is a mistake because if you don't have the lower body strength to produce force, you won't have any power behind these throws. Once your core and legs are strong, you'll be able to generate enough power to benefit from doing rotational medicine ball throws.

Let's get something straight: baseball specific training is NOT trying to mimic your swing or throwing motion with weights in the gym. Instead, baseball specific training refers to special strength exercises, like rotational medicine ball throws, that closely mimic the sporting action and speed seen in the baseball swing and throw.

When you do rotational medicine ball throws, the goal isn't to practice your swing or throwing motion. Instead, you are performing an explosive rotational movement that trains the body in the same plane in which you swing. You should not try to replicate your swing or throwing mechanics when doing these throws!

So to put this all together, increasing bat speed starts with building your foundation - your lower body and core. If you don't have your foundation in place but you're working on just increasing your rotational power with medicine ball throws, you're missing the boat and you won't get the results you are seeking.

It's kind of like studying high school material when you still haven't passed middle school. There's a time and place for baseball-specific exercises but you need to earn your right to do them. This is why strength training is so important for baseball players - you need your foundation in place before you try to build upon it.

Best Strength Exercises To Improve Bat Speed And Hitting Power

So now that you understand the importance of proper strength training for baseball, let's get into the specifics. Often baseball players will focus on the "beach muscles" or the ones you can see in the mirror, like the chest or biceps, but these aren't the muscles that make you a better baseball player.

If you were to look in the mirror, all the muscles that you can't see are the ones that require focus. This is also known as your posterior chain and includes your hamstrings, glutes, lower back and mid and upper back. These are the muscles that help produce hitting power and force.

The best exercises will depend on many factors, like the age of the athlete and the level of the athlete, but generally speaking for most baseball players, these are the five best exercises:

5 – Push-ups

Most people think push-ups are "too easy" and only train the upper body. The truth is proper push-ups not only utilize the upper body musculature but the entire body. Push-ups will demonstrate your ability to control your own bodyweight, which is critical to changing directions and running faster. Simply put, the better you control your body, the faster you will be able to run and change directions in the field. The key isn't just doing push-ups, you have to do them properly with perfect technique.

4 – Chin-ups (Pull-ups)

Similar to push-ups, pull-ups are a bodyweight exercise that will demonstrate your relative body strength, or how well you control your own bodyweight. If you increase the amount of proper chin-ups you can do, chances are you will also run faster and be able to change directions quicker. Chin-ups are also a great exercise that strengthens the upper back.

3 – Front Squats

The front squat is a great exercise that will help strengthen the lower body and core while also improving mobility. Unlike back squats, front squats put more pressure on your core and less on your back making it a more effective exercise for baseball players.

2 – Trap Bar Deadlifts

Trap bar deadlifts are a great posterior chain exercise that will strengthen your glutes, hamstrings and lower back. This exercise is easier to teach than many other posterior chain exercises; it offers a great bang for the buck.

1 – Reverse Lunges

Single leg exercises are critical for baseball players because they will help iron out imbalances from side to side. They will also improve hip mobility and stability, which will contribute to a stronger and more functional lower body.

Are you interested in training at GameChanger? Call us directly at (908) 376-9002 to get your free, no obligation, assessment for your son.

Or email me at Joe@GameChangerGym.com for more information on how we can help your son.

Chapter 3: How To Increase Velocity

" As a pitcher, you need to have a strong core"
- Craig Kimbrel

A major part of almost every coach's player assessment is throwing velocity. In fact, throwing velocity could be what's holding you back from reaching the next level, whether it's a starting spot on the varsity team, a college scholarship, or getting drafted. Coaches and scouts love velocity and use it as an important indicator of a pitcher's potential.

Luckily, the same principles and steps I talked about to increase bat speed, apply to increasing velocity. Even though hitting and throwing are two separate skills, you utilize the same musculature and you must display power in the same plane of motion. In a nutshell, the same fundamentals that will increase bat speed and hitting power will increase throwing velocity.

Imagine you're a pitcher and you're going through your windup. The windup starts with your legs – which are responsible for generating the power. As you move through your windup, the power your legs generate is transmitted through your core to the upper body and then projected onto the baseball.

In order to increase velocity you need to make this process more efficient. While your throwing and pitching mechanics have a major part to do with this, you certainly can increase your velocity with proper strength training if you focus on these five key areas:

1 – Increase Lower Body Strength

The lower body is a major part of the foundation for pitching. You have to have a strong, stable and functional foundation of lower body strength to support and increase throwing velocity. Remember, your legs are like an engine, the more horsepower or strength you can get out of the engine, the more powerful the engine will be.

2 – Increase Core Strength

The core is responsible for power transfer and protecting the spine. In order to train the core properly, you need to focus on exercises that improve the stability of your core. The best types of core exercises are those that increase your core's ability to resist movement. If we have a weak core, we're going to have a leakage of power and energy through the kinetic chain. So the key is to focus on exercises that improve core stability.

3 – Strengthen Your Decelerating Muscles

The decelerating muscles are the muscles in the back of your shoulder that slow your arm down after you release the baseball. Strengthening these muscles is critical because you can only throw as fast as you can slow your arm down. For example, let's say I told you to stand fifty (50) feet from a wall and I told you to run as fast as you can, would you: (A) run through the wall at top speed or (B) slow your body down so you don't go crashing into the wall. There's a good chance you will select option B.

The same concept is applied to the throwing motion. If your body knows it can't slow your arm down, it's not going to let you accelerate your arm to its maximum capability because it can't slow it down. What good is a Ferrari if you don't have the brakes to slow it down? The great part about this is that if you just improve your decelerating strength, there are miles per hour that are already inside of you!

4 – Increase Rotational Power

Like we mentioned earlier, your ability to create rotational power will directly impact your bat speed and throwing velocity. The best way to achieve this is through rotational medicine ball throws once you build up a solid foundation of lower body and core strength.

5 – Increase your Athleticism

The more athletic you are, the easier it will be for you to make mechanical adjustments that will put you in a better position to throw harder. If you don't have good athleticism, it doesn't matter how strong you are if you cannot get into the proper mechanical position to display your strength.

Are you interested in training at GameChanger?
Call us directly at (908) 376-9002 to get
your free, no obligation, assessment for your son.

Or email me at Joe@GameChangerGym.com
for more information on how
we can help your son.

Best Exercises To Improve Throwing Velocity

While all the exercises to improve bat speed will also help with velocity, I'll share with you five more exercises that will improve throwing velocity.

1 – Band Pull Apart

The band pull apart is a great exercise that will strengthen the decelerating muscles of the upper back.

2 – Abdominal Wheel Rollouts

Abdominal wheel rollouts are a great exercise to strengthen the anterior core.

3 – Single Leg RDL (Romanian Deadlift)

Single leg RDLs are a very challenging exercise that will strengthen the posterior chain as well as improve your stability.

4 – Rotational Shot Put Throw

Rotational shot put throws are an excellent exercise to develop rotational power.

5 – Rotational Medicine Ball Slams

Rotational medicine ball slams are another great exercise to develop rotational power specific to the throwing motion.

Chapter 4: Speed Training For Baseball

"People say I stole a lot of bases. I stole the bases for a reason. I crossed the plate."
— Ricky Henderson

You've heard the expression "speed skills" haven't you? In the game of baseball, speed will have a large impact on the outcome of the game. From an offensive perspective, the faster players on the team will beat out slow rollers in the infield, steal more bases, avoid double plays, stretch singles into doubles and doubles into triples, and will score more runs.

From a defensive perspective, the faster players on the team will have better range to track down fly balls than the slower ones or to field balls in the hole that the slower players can't get to. Speed will allow you to save extra bases and runs because you'll hold runners by getting the ball back to the cutoff man and infielder faster.

There's no wonder why one of the most common questions baseball parents ask is, "What does my son need to do to get faster?" Getting faster comes down to this - if you want to get faster you have to focus on producing more force. The more force you put to the ground, the faster you're going to run.

Let's go back to the car analogy. The more horsepower you can get out of the engine, the faster the car will go. In order to produce more force, or get more horsepower out of the engine, there are five keys baseball players need to focus on.

Five Keys To Getting Faster

Key # 1 – Increase Lower Body Strength

Getting faster starts from the ground up and begins with building your foundation. By strengthening your lower body, more specifically the muscles of the posterior chain, you will be able to produce more force and run faster. Strong legs are the key to running faster.

Key # 2 – Increase Your Rate Of Force Development

Once you have a solid base of lower body strength, you'll want to add in explosive lower body training like jumps and sprints to improve the rate at which you develop force. Jumping and sprinting will make you explosive, but you need to be smart about how you implement these exercises.

When it comes to how many jumps and sprints to do, more isn't always better. In fact, more quantity will lead to decreased performance. Instead, focus on quality technique and being as explosive as possible.

Key # 3 – Increase Your Ability To Decelerate

The key to a fast car is great brakes. What good is it to drive a Ferrari if you don't have the brakes to slow it down? Like the arm, you can only run as fast as you can slow your body down. Not only will improving deceleration help you run faster, it will also help prevent lower body injuries.

Key # 4 – Increase Relative Body Strength

How strong you are relative to your body weight is critical to running faster. Often times I can tell how fast a baseball player is by just watching him move and perform simple bodyweight exercises. For example, pushups, pull-ups, lunges and squats are foundational movements that show how well you handle your own bodyweight.

Way too often, baseball players will overlook the importance of mastering their own bodyweight. Instead they look for external tools like weighted vests, parachutes and agility ladders to get faster. This is a big mistake. If you want to get faster, don't worry about using fancy tools. Instead, focus on becoming a master of your own bodyweight.

If you become great at doing perfect push-ups, pull-ups, squats and lunges, you will get faster! In all of my experience, the baseball players that master these exercises will be faster than baseball players who struggle with these exercises.

Key # 5 – Improve Core Strength

Earlier I spoke about the importance of core strength when it comes to increasing velocity and hitting power. The core is also critical to improving your speed. The role of the core in running is to transfer force from the lower body through the entire kinetic chain. In other words, when you are running, your foot strikes the ground, which produces force.

This force is then transferred from your lower body across the hips and into the upper body. If you have a weak core, you won't be able to effectively transfer this force and you'll have energy leakage. In a nutshell, a weak core will hold you back from reaching your full speed potential.

Three Speed Training Mistakes Exposed

Mistake # 1 – Using The Speed And Agility Ladder To Get Faster

The speed and agility ladder is a popular tool used by many coaches with the goal of improving foot speed. While it's a good tool for young athletes to improve coordination and basic footwork, the agility ladder will not make a more advanced athlete faster.

If we lined up two major leaguers next to each other and had them race to first base who do you think would win: Player A, who took more strides or Player B, who took less strides? Player B would win the race because each stride he takes is more powerful, producing more force and propelling him forward faster.

Player A needs to take more frequent strides because he can't produce as much force with each foot strike compared to Player B. Even though his feet are moving faster, he's not going as far. In other words, getting faster doesn't have to do with having "quick feet". In fact, quick feet can actually slow you down because you aren't effectively using all your power. So ditch the agility ladder and focus on the five keys we talked about above.

Mistake # 2 – Running Too Much

There are two common mistakes when it comes to running too much. The first mistake is the idea that long distance running will make you faster. Sprinting is explosive. You're not going to get faster and more explosive by running very slow for long distances. The body doesn't work that way.

The second mistake baseball players make is turning their speed sessions into conditioning and endurance training. Real speed training requires a lot less volume or distance then you might think.

According to the great speed coach, Charlie Francis, your entire speed workout should be no more then 300 total yards. This means ten (10) 30-yard sprints are more than enough. The same concepts should be applied to jumps and medicine ball throws. When it comes to getting faster, more isn't always better. Instead, focus on quality over quantity.

Mistake # 3 – Not Resting Long Enough

Another common mistake is not resting fully in between sprints. Let's say the workout calls for ten (10) 30-yard sprints but you decide to jog back between each sprint and then sprint again – this isn't speed training because you are not fully recovered.

Instead you are training for conditioning and endurance. In order to get faster, you have to fully rest in between sprints. So don't make the mistake of doing conditioning if your goal is to get faster.

Agility And Change Of Direction Training

Agility and change of direction are critical in baseball. Whether you're fielding a ground ball in the hole, tracking down a ball in the gap or running the bases, you must be agile and you must be able to change direction quickly. Below are five surefire ways to improve your agility and change of direction ability.

1 - Improve Your Positional Skills

Many baseball critics think of Robinson Cano as being lazy in the field. While he may not always run hard around the bases, when it comes to his defense, the truth is he's a master of his skills because he is very fluid with his movements. These fluid movements give the impression that he's nonchalant, but the truth is when you master your skills, you're going to make them look easier than a player who doesn't have the same skill set as you.

Why is agility important to improving a player's positional skills? When you improve your skills, you will be able to react quicker to balls off the bat and thus make sure you are in the proper fielding position.

www.GameChangerGym.com

The same concepts apply to other areas of your game as well. If you want to run the bases better, you need to practice your base running skills. If you're an outfielder, you need to practice on getting great reads off the bat. This is how you improve your agility.

I'm sure you can think of a base runner that isn't the fastest guy on the team but he is still a great base runner. He possesses good baseball speed, which means he has great instincts. For example, he gets great jumps on balls in the dirt or line drives in the gap. When it comes to stealing bases, he chooses his spots wisely.

2 - Improve Your Ability to Decelerate

If you have to make sharp cuts and turns on the field, you must be able to absorb and redirect forces quickly and effectively. This comes down to your ability to slow your body down, or decelerate, and then accelerate again. Simply put, the better your brakes, the quicker you will be able to change direction.

3 - Improve Your Acceleration

Improving your ability to accelerate is critical to being more agile and changing direction quickly. In order to improve your acceleration, refer to the five key tips to getting faster that I mentioned earlier in this chapter.

4 - Improve Your Relative Body Strength

Improving relative body strength will help you make more powerful contractions when your foot strikes the ground. These more powerful contractions are going to propel you forward and help you accelerate. Focus on becoming a master of your bodyweight and you will see that you'll have much better body control and be able to move much quicker on the baseball diamond.

5 - Field Your Position In Batting Practice

The issue with cone drills, agility ladders and other agility drills is the fact that they are predicable. When it comes to baseball and playing your position, you don't know if the ball is going to go five feet to your right or to your left – it's unpredictable.

There's no better way to improve your agility on the baseball field then improving your skills as a defender. The best time to do this is in batting practice because it's totally unpredictable. Even in most practices, you know when and where the coach is going to hit the ball, but the same can't be said about batting practice. You need to treat each of these reps like it's the last out of the World Series.

To wrap it up, increasing your speed and agility comes down to putting more horsepower in the engine with proper strength training and training your nervous system with sprints, medicine ball throws and jumps. Don't forget you also need to have the brakes in place to slow you down. If you have a Ferrari engine but no brakes, you won't ever be able to use the engine's full capability.

Lastly, understand that getting faster and more agile is a process. There's no magic drill that's going to make your faster. You have to work on all these aspects if you want to get faster!

Chapter 5: Exactly What Age Should My Son Begin Strength Training?

"I was probably 12 or 13 when I started doing pushups, situps, dips." – Bryce Harper

Let's get something straight, I understand your concern for your child's health and safety. You want your son to get faster, more agile and stronger but you don't want to compromise his health or risk an injury, and you certainly don't want to stunt his growth. So to answer the question "exactly what age should my son begin strength training?" – you are never too young to understand how to handle your own bodyweight.

When parents think of strength training, they often think of barbells and plates. The truth is proper strength training for youth athletes doesn't mean using barbells and plates. Instead, proper strength training for youth athletes starts with mastering your own bodyweight.

"The scientific literature is quite clear that strength training is safe for young people, if it's properly supervised,"
- Dr. Faigenbaum

At GameChanger Strength & Performance, we start training athletes as young as nine years old because this is the best age to teach an athlete a new skill. At this age they learn these new skills and absorb them like a sponge. This lays the foundation for later in life when they are ready to lift weights. Also, bodyweight training at this age will actually help prevent injury which is the # 1 goal of any training program.

We utilize bodyweight training with all our athletes once they join our program. There are a few reasons why I love bodyweight training. Number one, it's totally safe and it's suitable for little leaguers, ball players just stepping onto the 60/90 field for the first time, high school athletes and even college and pro baseball players. So bodyweight training is totally safe for baseball players of any age.

Bodyweight training is scalable and versatile. You don't need any fancy or expensive equipment and you can do it from the comfort of your own home, at the park, or even at the baseball field. Bodyweight training is great for team training because it gives the coach the flexibility to have middle school and high school baseball players work together and get equally challenging workouts.

Bodyweight training will help improve your performance. It will improve your coordination and proprioception, which are important to improving your movement, reaction ability, agility, speed and overall athleticism. Proper bodyweight training will improve your relative body strength – how well you handle your own bodyweight.

The better you handle your own bodyweight, the faster you will run, the more explosive you will be, and the more agile you will be. And that's why we always start our athletes off with bodyweight training and only progress them when they have earned their right to do so.

Think about this - many parents have no problem with their son playing baseball year round, throwing curveballs before they know how to locate a fastball, taking hundreds of swings a week or even playing a contact sport like football where they are getting tackled and butting heads. But many of these same parents do have a problem with proper strength training using your own bodyweight. This is problematic.

This may not be something you want to hear, but throwing a baseball is much more dangerous to the body than doing a proper bodyweight exercise. Throwing a baseball is the single fastest motion in all of sports. Many youth athletes aren't prepared to handle the demands they place on their bodies from playing year round baseball. If you're not physically fit to do something, eventually you're going to get injured (Side note: I will cover this more in-depth in the next chapter).

But let's go back to strength training for a minute - anything done improperly is going to be dangerous. But the idea that strength training in general is dangerous for youth baseball players is just flat out wrong. If you are following an age appropriate program using your own bodyweight, and have proper coaching, you are actually going to prevent injury while laying the foundation for your future success. This is why it's critical to get your son involved in a proper strength-training program that focuses on bodyweight movements as soon as you can.

Chapter 6: Injury Prevention For Baseball

"Specialization leads to playing the sport year-round. That means not only an increase in risk factors for traumatic injuries but a sky-high increase in overuse injuries."
– Dr. James Andrews

Let's face facts. Injuries in youth baseball are happening now more than ever before from overuse. According to the American Orthopedic Society for Sports Medicine (AOSSM), "since 2000, there has been a fivefold increase in the number of serious shoulder and elbow injuries among youth baseball players." The number one reason for this is overuse. With the rise of travel teams, showcases, fall ball and winter baseball, kids today are playing baseball more than ever before and year round baseball is becoming the standard.

If you're not playing baseball all year round or if you're not playing for multiple teams during the spring and summer, you're falling behind. Since many parents and coaches think that more baseball is better; it shouldn't be a surprise that there has been a five-time increase in elbow and shoulder injuries since the year 2000.

When it comes to injuries, it's not the one pitch that is thrown or the one game where too many pitches were thrown that cause an injury. Instead, it's an accumulation of all the little things that add up and cause an injury. That one game or that one pitch is the straw that broke the camel's back. Let's use our car analogy again. The more wear and tear and miles you put on the car, the more likely it is to break down. The same principle applies to your arm and throwing. The more mileage you put on your arm, the more at risk you will be for an injury, especially if you accumulate these miles at such a young age.

Another issue with playing year round baseball is that all you are doing is testing your skills. If all you're doing is testing your skills by playing more games, you're never going to become a better baseball player. You need to take the time to make adjustments and work on your mechanics. You can't do this when you are always testing your skills. You need to take the time to build your skills.

Think of this analogy - if your son only took tests in school all the time and never took the time to prepare, practice and study for these tests, how do you think he would do? Chances are he would do poorly because he never had the time to properly prepare. How would he ever get smarter if he were just testing the skills he already possesses? The same thing can be said for baseball.

If your son is just playing games year round and he's not taking the time to develop his skills and improve his physical fitness, he will never maximize his potential as a baseball player. He needs to take the time to work with his hitting or pitching coach and develop as an athlete. From experience, I know how hard it is to make an adjustment in the middle of the season, especially now that kids are playing over one hundred (100) games in a calendar year.

Not only is playing year round baseball leaving a player vulnerable to injury, but from a developmental standpoint, you can't develop if all you're doing is testing the skills you already have. It's impossible to develop new skills that way.

Basically there is no off-season, many baseball players are in-season year round. That's why so many kids get burned out and why they're peaking at such a young age. People think that strength training is dangerous but really, if you're a baseball player, the most dangerous thing you can do is play baseball all year around.

Four Surefire Ways To Prevent Injuries

Injury Prevention Tip # 1 - Take Time Off From Throwing

Parents often ask me, "What are the best exercises to prevent arm injuries?" My advice always is to take time off from throwing during certain times of the year and to play a second sport. This is not something that baseball parents often want to hear, but it's the truth. And I know from experience because growing up I played baseball all year round and I've always dealt with arm issues.

Injury Prevention Tip # 2 - Improve Your Mechanics As A Pitcher

If you're pitching and you have bad mechanics, every pitch you throw is going to cause more wear and tear compared to a pitcher with good mechanics. If you improve your mechanics it's going to help with your ability to prevent injury and it's also going to make you a better pitcher. If you improve your pitching mechanics not only is it going to help you throw harder, it's also going to help you be more efficient with your delivery and it's going to help you prevent injury.

Injury Prevention Tip # 3 - Improve Your Physical Fitness And Athleticism

The other way to prevent injuries is to improve your physical fitness and athleticism. Many kids today are out of shape but yet they are running down the first baseline as fast as they can, or they are running from first to third. It's no wonder why kids are getting injured – their bodies are not physically prepared to do what they are demanding of them. You don't get in shape by playing baseball, instead you need to be in shape to play baseball.

Injury Prevention Tip # 4 - Warm-Up Properly

If you are not warming-up properly before games and practices, you're going to be more vulnerable to an injury. A good warm-up does not consist of jogging a few laps and some static stretches. Although this is the typical baseball warm-up, this kind of regimen is not effective for preventing injuries.

Instead, baseball players should do a full-body dynamic warm up. The goal of the warm-up is to increase blood flow, activate and mobilize the muscles that you're going to use, increase core body temperature, break a light sweat and improve movement quality. Not only will this physically prepare you to play baseball at your peak performance, but it will also help bullet proof your body from injuries.

Chapter 7: In-Season Training For Baseball

Physically, you have to prepare your body to be in the best shape possible until the end of October, because that is when I plan to stop playing each season. -Albert Pujols

Most baseball players overlook the importance of proper in-season strength training. One of the biggest mistakes baseball players make is working their butts off in the off-season only to stop training once the season starts. This is a huge mistake, because when you stop training during the season you'll start to see your performance drop off. You'll notice that your velocity will decrease, you'll start missing with your fastball high and in or low and away and you won't be able to locate your pitches the way you want.

The reason why this happens is as the season goes on, your body starts to break down and you actually get weaker if you're not training properly. The baseball players that train at GameChanger during the baseball season actually get stronger as the season goes on.

Their velocity increases and they are getting stronger while their competition gets weaker. Our baseball players are hitting their peak for the most important games of the year when their teams need them the most. Mentally they stay strong and they have the confidence to compete against anyone because they know nobody is outworking them. This is exactly why you need to train during the baseball season.

If you want to become the best baseball player you can be, you have to be willing to do what other baseball players aren't willing to do. Every baseball player is playing games, taking batting practice and practicing baseball skills.

But what most baseball players are overlooking, especially in-season, is proper in-season strength training. In-season training will be the game changer for you. It's what will separate you from everyone else. While your competition starts to break down and get weaker, you will be getting stronger.

Most baseball players will make excuses like, "I don't have time to train in-season," "I'm too tired," or "the workouts are too hard." If this is the way you think, then you need to change your attitude because you're lying to yourself. If you don't think there's enough time to train, it's because you're not making the time.

If you're too tired, then you need to focus on recovery, regeneration and nutrition. How are you fueling your body? How are you sleeping? These are all factors that will affect your energy. If your workouts are too hard then you need to change them up by making them shorter and less intense; most importantly, you need to start listening to your body.

Seven In-Season Training Tips

There are a few fundamental changes you need to make when training in-season. Below are seven ways in-season workouts differ from off-season workouts:

In-Season Training Tip # 1 - Do Shorter Workouts

In-season workouts should be shorter compared to your off-season workouts. The ideal time for an in-season workout is 30-45 minutes. This is just enough time to get into the gym do your recovery and regeneration work and your strength training.

In-Season Training Tip # 2 - Focus More On Recovery

If you want to feel good during the season and avoid injury, you have to take care of your body. You cannot neglect the importance of soft tissue work and proper mobility training in-season. This should be prioritized in your in-season workouts.

In-Season Training Tip # 3 - Do Less Volume

During the season you don't need to do as many sets and reps compared to the off-season. Instead of doing 3 x 10, try doing 3 x 6 or 3 x 8; less volume equals less soreness.

In-Season Training Tip # 4 - Do Exercises You Are Familiar With

During the season is not the right time to introduce exercises you never did before, because we want to limit soreness. New exercises will tend to make you sore and for this reason, the best time to introduce new exercises is in the off-season when you aren't playing baseball everyday.

In-Season Training Tip # 5 - Listen To Your Body

The key to your success during the season is to listen to your body. There will be days when you feel great and you can train a little harder. There will be days when you are physically and/or mentally tired and you need to take it easy with the weights and focus more on mobility and soft tissue work.

In-Season Training Tip # 6 - Do Less Eccentric Exercises

The eccentric part of an exercise is the part where you're lowering the weight down. For example, in a push-up, pull-up or squat, the eccentric phase is when you lower your body. This is the part of the exercise that gets you sore. In order to reduce soreness, we want to add in some exercises that don't require any eccentric lowering. One of our favorite tools to utilize in-season is the sled.

In Season Training Tip # 7 - Do Less Speed, Agility and Conditioning

Playing baseball consists of speed, agility and conditioning. Instead of doing this in-season, focus on strength training because this is one area that does not get addressed by playing your sport.

What Results Can You Get During The Season?

Another common question a parent may ask is, "what results will my son get when training in-season?" When I opened up GameChanger Strength & Performance in May of 2013, all of the baseball players that joined the program were in the middle of their seasons and within weeks they started to see awesome results. They started to see gains in velocity, speed around the bases, and in bat speed. They were getting stronger as their competition was getting weaker.

If you're more advanced, it's obviously going to be harder to see these types of gains in-season when you can't train as hard, but for the younger baseball player or for the baseball player that doesn't start everyday, you should expect to see these types of results with proper in-season training.

Sample In-Season Training Program

Phase 1: Soft Tissue Work

During this part of the workout we utilize tools like foam rollers and lacrosse balls to help soften up the muscle tissue to get rid of knots, adhesions, and scar tissue that are caused from throwing and being active and being an athlete.

Phase 2: Dynamic Warm-up

The goal of our warm-up is to increase core temperature, break a sweat, mobilize the ankles, hips and thoracic spine and activate the muscles we are going to use during the session.

Phase 3: C.N.S. (Central Nervous System) Activation

The goal of phase 3 is to get your body primed to train, to get you more alert so you can perform at your best.

Phase 4: Strength Training

This will depend on the age of the athlete, the level of the athlete, their schedule and how they feel.

Phase 5: Regeneration and Recovery

The goal of each in-season workout is to leave the gym feeling better than when you came in.

Are you interested in training at GameChanger?
Call us directly at (908) 376-9002 to get
your free, no obligation, assessment for your son.

Or email me at Joe@GameChangerGym.com
for more information on how
we can help your son.

Chapter 8: What Lifts Should Baseball Players Never Do?

"Legs are probably the most important thing to focus on in all sports." – Derek Jeter

When it comes to exercise selection for baseball players, you always have to weigh the risk vs. the reward. You should never do an exercise where the risk is greater than the reward. For many baseball players, this includes exercises that stress the shoulder joint by putting it in a vulnerable position.

1 - The Military Press

If you're beating your shoulder up playing baseball, the last thing you need to do is beat it up even more in the gym and put more stress on it from bench pressing and overhead pressing.

2 - The Bench Press

While the bench press is a great lift for many athletes, when it comes to baseball specifically, the reward is not worth the risk. Baseball players can get the results the bench press provides in much safer exercises like push-ups and dumbbell bench presses.

3 - Olympic Lifts

Olympic lifting is a sport in itself. The lifts are complex and hard to learn. There are much better ways for baseball players to get more explosive that are easier to learn including jumps, medicine ball throws and sprints.

4 - Back Squat

Back squats are generally a great exercise but I don't recommend them to baseball players. The back squat places the shoulder in a vulnerable position. Instead, baseball players should do front squats because they are much easier on the shoulder and back.

5 - Machine Leg Extension

The machine leg extension is a popular exercise among bodybuilders to increase the size of their quads but it's a non-functional exercise that provides no benefit to baseball players.

6 - Machine Leg Curl

Similar to the leg extension, the machine leg curl is a non-functional exercise that offers little benefit to baseball players.

7 - Leg Press

The leg press is a good exercise to increase lower body strength but unlike the squat, the leg press does not improve core stability. This is why many athletes can leg press more then they can squat.

8 - Dips

Dips are a great exercise to increase the size of the shoulders, chest and triceps but it puts the shoulder in a vulnerable position, making it a bad choice for baseball players.

9 - Chest Fly

The chest fly is an exercise that targets the chest muscles but doesn't offer any athletic benefit to baseball players. Instead, baseball players would be better off doing push-ups because they train the entire body and allow the scapula to move freely.

10 - Upright Row

The upright row should be avoided at all costs by baseball players. This exercise will only do harm and offers no benefit to athletic performance.

Are you interested in training at GameChanger?
Call us directly at (908) 376-9002 to get
your free, no obligation, assessment for your son.

Or email me at Joe@GameChangerGym.com
for more information on how
we can help your son.

Chapter 9: Six Baseball Training Myths Exposed

"During my first 3 years in the AL, I pitched more than 900 innings. There's no way I could have recovered quickly, or been as durable, without a firm base of strength from lifting. Lifting helped me be more consistent." - Nolan Ryan

Myth # 1 - Baseball Players Should Run Long Distance

Many coaches believe that running poles or long distance is the key to improving stamina and will also help improve velocity. This is a myth that has been accepted at almost every level of baseball. Baseball is a power sport. It is a game of quick, short, and explosive bursts.

While a high aerobic capacity is needed to maintain heat in the muscles as the game goes on, long distance running is not the answer because the lactic acid loads are too great. In other words, long distance running is detrimental to baseball performance because it will interfere with your ability to recover. Instead of conditioning like cross-country runners, baseball players should condition like sprinters.

Myth # 2 - Agility Ladders & Cone Drills Will Make You Faster

Most coaches and players think that by simply using an agility ladder or cone drills that an athlete will become more agile. Many strength and conditioning coaches will try to impress you by doing these fancy agility ladder drills. Unfortunately, this is all show and no go.

The problem with these drills is the fact that they are predetermined. In a baseball game, you don't know which direction you are going to have to move to track down a fly ball, field a ground ball, or block a wild pitch. Baseball is unpredictable. The other issue with these drills is that they don't improve force development, which is the key to running faster and being more agile.

If you want to become a more agile, explosive and powerful baseball player, you need to improve the rate you can display force quickly. This all starts with building a solid foundation of strength. Once this foundation is built, you can then improve force development with more reactive training like sprints, medicine ball throws and jumps. There's no magic drill when it comes to speed training, you have to focus on just becoming a better athlete, producing more force, and the speed will come.

Myth # 3 - Baseball Players Shouldn't Lift Weights

Baseball is a ballistic sport that involves quick and explosive movements. In order to increase power and speed, you must have a solid base and foundation to build on.

Stronger baseball players who are able to produce forceful contractions will be more successful than weaker players who rely on skill only. The combination of skill, power and strength will help baseball players reach their maximum potential.

Are you interested in training at GameChanger?
Call us directly at (908) 376-9002 to get
your free, no obligation, assessment for your son.

Or email me at Joe@GameChangerGym.com
for more information on how
we can help your son.

Myth # 4 - You Need To Play Baseball Games All Year Round To Get Better

Common sense would tell you that if you want to get better at baseball, you should play games all year around. The problem is, when all you do is play games, you are only testing your skills, and you cannot build or improve them.

Like I mentioned earlier, if your teacher gave you a test every week, without giving you the opportunity to learn the material, how well do you think you would do? This is exactly what happens when you play games all year. It's very hard to work on making adjustments in your throwing mechanics or in your swing when you are constantly playing games.

Don't get me wrong, competing is important but competing year round isn't worth the wear and tear you will place on your arm and/or your body. There needs to be a balance between developing the proper skill set and displaying it on the field.

Myth # 5 - Leaving A Workout Tired Is An Indication Of A Good Workout

Many baseball players think that they need to vomit or feel extremely tired after a workout to get results. A smart strength and conditioning coach understands that being tired is not an indication of a good workout. Instead, a better indication of a "good" workout is how you are progressing from week to week.

Are you getting stronger, faster, and more explosive? How do you feel physically and mentally? How is it carrying over to your game on the baseball field? These are the questions you want to ask yourself after a workout to judge whether or not what you are doing is effective.

While training hard is important, it's more important to train smart. The blend of training smart and hard is the ultimate combination to becoming a better baseball player. This is why finding an experienced strength and conditioning coach who can take all the guesswork out of the equation for you is critical. You don't need to worry about all the little nuances that go into designing and implementing a training program, all you have to do is put in the work!

Myth # 6 - Arm Care Exercises Alone Will Prevent Arm Injuries

Many coaches think that doing just band exercises from various angles will prevent injuries. When you throw a baseball you utilize your entire body. With this said, you're going to need a lot more then a strong rotator cuff to prevent injury. This is why you need to have a foundation of strength and athleticism, especially in your lower half and core. Simply put, pitchers who are stronger and more athletic will do a better job at decelerating their arm compared to those pitchers that just focus on band exercises for the rotator cuff.

Chapter 10: How To Choose A Baseball Specific Strength & Conditioning Program For Your Child

"You never know when more responsibility will come. But big things happen to those who hustle. Show up every day and bust your hump, and people will not only respect you but start relying on you, too." – Jacoby Ellsbury

If you are thinking about hiring a strength and conditioning coach, I offer these four recommendations:

Recommendation # 1: Make a commitment to your child and invest in a quality strength and conditioning coach as soon as possible. The longer you wait to hire a strength and conditioning coach, the more your child will fall behind and will have a bigger disadvantage against his competition.

High school baseball players have a very short window of opportunity to make the most out of their career. Those who make the most out of it, go on to play at the next level.

Recommendation # 2: List your objectives. Do you want your child to train at the typical training facility where they get mediocre to average results? Or do you want your child to get the best results possible by sending him to a results focused training facility that guarantees results, like ours.

Recommendation # 3: Ask questions. The best way for you to determine whether or not the strength and conditioning coach you are hiring is experienced is to ask specific questions and to listen carefully to the answers. Here are just a few questions I suggest you ask:

1) Do you have written success stories from your previous baseball players?

2) How many days a week do you recommend training for my child?

3) What is your training philosophy when it comes to training baseball players?

4) What training and experience do you have in training athletes?

5) What type of training do you do during each session?

Recommendation # 4: Once you have found a strength and conditioning coach that you think will provide the best results for your child, ask to sign up for a free assessment. During this free assessment, the strength and conditioning coach should tell you exactly what your child's strengths are, as well as their areas of improvement, and what type of results your child can expect from joining his or her strength and conditioning program.

By following the information in this guide, you will be able to make an informed decision when choosing a strength and conditioning coach. If you want to hire a cheap, inexperienced coach, I'm sure there are plenty of low-cost options available in your area. But if you want to give your child top notch coaching by a team of true professionals and get him involved in a complete strength and conditioning program - increasing strength, power, speed, explosiveness, while adding lean muscle and improving mobility and flexibility - then I invite you to call me.

I'll be happy to answer your questions - tell you how our membership works - or to schedule your child for a free assessment - without obligation of any kind. To reach me, call our facility 908-376-9002 and ask for Joe Meglio or, if you prefer, just e-mail me at Joe@gamechangergym.com and I will be happy to answer your questions.

Here's one last point: I know that many parents are skeptical about getting their sons involved in a strength and conditioning program. Before I got into this business, I was skeptical too. So in addition to providing this educational material, I will do one more thing: I will guarantee my work. That's right, I fully guarantee the results your child will achieve. If you aren't completely satisfied with the results your child obtains, I'll refund you every single penny.

As a matter of fact, add this additional question to the list above: (6) "Do you guarantee your work?" Not all coaches do and it's important that you have this information before you make your decision. Thank you very much for reading the *Parents Guide To Strength Training For Baseball*.

Are you interested in training at GameChanger?
Call us directly at (908) 376-9002 to get
your free, no obligation, assessment for your son.

Or email me at Joe@GameChangerGym.com
for more information on how
we can help your son.

About the Author

Joe Meglio is the owner of GameChanger Strength & Performance in Union County, New Jersey. Joe is also a former college baseball player and has been featured on ESPN Page 2, Paul Reddick Baseball, STACK Magazine and Elite FTS.

He is a co-author of an Amazon best selling book *No Gym, No Time, No Problem.* Over the past 5 years Joe has worked with hundreds of local baseball players through the Yogi Berra Museum, various travel baseball teams and high school baseball teams. Joe has helped thousands of baseball players, coaches and parents from all over the county through his online baseball training manuals, courses and books.

Joe also was named the first ever STACK.com Expert of the Month and in 2011 he was voted the # 1 Rising Star in the Fitness Industry by Fitnessbusiness-interviews.com

In 2014, Joe was a featured speaker at the Ohio High School Baseball Coaches Association, the second largest High School Coaches Association in the U.S. At the clinic, Joe spoke alongside some of the biggest Division 1 Coaches in college baseball including: Scott Strickland of the University of Georgia, Ty Neil of the University of Cincinnati, Josh Newman of Marshall University, Greg Beals of the Ohio State University, Steve Trimper of the University of Maine and former head coach Bob Morgan of Indiana University.

Praise For GameChanger

"His passion for his sport has grown as a result of this training…"

"The results have been unbelievable since he started. Brian has gained 23lbs to date! His strength behind his bat has improved tremendously & his passion for his sport has grown as a result of this training!"

– Ann Henn, from Union, NJ.

"I wanted to find my son the best in class program around & GameChanger has been the perfect fit…"

"As a parent, who has a son that sets high standards for himself, I wanted to find him the best in class program around & GameChanger has been the perfect fit. GameChanger provides a great environment that is results focused & fosters camaraderie with their athletes while continuing to push & challenge them further than they think they can go."

-*Joe* Bonaccorso, from Scotch Plains, NJ

"...He became more confident because he knows that he can hit the ball harder and run faster than other kids..."

My son Tyler, who is almost 15, started training with GameChanger Strength & Performance in December of 2012. Tyler needed to adjust to the big field when he turned 13 and Joe was just the person who could provide training to be stronger, faster, more agile: all of which is essential to be a better baseball player. Tyler's batting coach, Bryan, referred him to Joe and he gave us expert advice and training catered specifically to the game of baseball.

We could not be happier now that we have witnessed a huge difference in Tyler on the field, physically and mentally. He became more confident because he knows that he can hit the ball harder and faster than other kids.

One more positive change that we noticed is how Tyler has much more stamina. So when he has to put in more time for homework, he doesn't get tired and inattentive that easily. I think this kind of training and discipline will carry him through all throughout his high school years and then more.

-Chan Lee from, from Basking Ridge, NJ

"...The program has made him a better athlete through strength training and the value of better nutrition..."

When Robert joined GameChanger, his goal was to get in better shape. He knew to compete at the high school level he needed to improve his speed, agility and strength. In short, the program has made him a better athlete through strength training and the value of better nutrition.

It also motivated him to work out on his own. Robert felt his primary position would be 3B in high school. But throughout the summer and fall seasons, Robert has played and is confident that he can play any position. This gives him a competitive edge going into the 2014 high school season.

-Jim Herron, from Springfield, NJ

"...He hit close to .400 with 7 doubles, 3 triples and 21 RBIs making this his best season of high school and was named team MVP award for his senior year..."

We first heard of Joe Meglio from a close friend and coach, Bryan Henton, who highly recommended him. We are really happy he did. My son Matt has been working with Joe for a little over 3 months and the results are unbelievable. Matt has gotten much stronger and more explosive in almost every aspect of his game. His hitting has improved greatly, he hits the ball much harder and farther, and his running has as well, he gets down the line much faster and quicker and seems to be stealing bases with ease.

During Matt's high school season, all the work he had put in with Joe Meglio and Bryan Henton showed greatly. He hit close to .400 with 7 doubles, 3 triples and 21 rbis making this his best season of high school. In addition we are very proud that he received the MVP award for his senior year.

Because of Joe my son has put on a good amount of muscle, Matt started off weighing close to 150 pounds, but in about 3 months he has been able to put on an incredible 13 pounds while still in season. Another important change that my wife and I have seen is how much more confident Matt became. We are truly happy that Joe has been able to work with our son and just make him a better athlete. Thank you Joe Meglio.

– Joe Marques from Union, New Jersey

"...The key difference between GameChanger and other "gyms" is that GameChanger is geared toward baseball with the involvement of likeminded baseball players..."

Since joining GameChanger, Kobi has been able to elevate his game to a new level in a relatively short period of time. He has become much stronger which has boosted his performance at the plate. The other aspect is more intangible and that is that Kobi has gained more confidence as a result of following a set routine with GameChanger. He is much more comfortable with his ability on the field, which has helped his team on a number of occasions win games.

GameChanger is a good environment for anyone that is serious about baseball. The key difference between GameChanger and other "gyms" is that GameChanger is geared toward baseball with the involvement of likeminded baseball players. I would encourage any player to give GameChanger a try!!!

– Greg Wolf from Westfield, NJ

"...Mike is currently playing up a year, and his training with GameChanger has helped greatly with being able to keep up and perform well with the older kids..."

In the short time Mike as been with GameChanger, he has seen a noticeable increase in his strength, speed and quickness. GameChanger has been different than other programs because their baseball specific workouts have done a much better job preparing Mike with the skills necessary to be successful on the diamond.

Mike is currently playing up a year, and his training with GameChanger has helped greatly with being able to keep up and perform well with the older kids. The training Joe and his staff provide at GameChanger is a great tool for any serious baseball player.

– Richard Baylor from Fanwood, NJ

"...The results have been amazing. Remy is stronger, leaner, faster but most of all his confidence is at an all-time high..."

My son Remy first started training with Joe in late January of 2012 for 8 weeks leading up to the high school season. Remy loved it so much that we began again in October 2012 and haven't stopped training yet. The results have been amazing. Remy is stronger, leaner, faster but most of all his confidence is at an all-time high. Joe has help build an inner belief of self-confidence that I have never seen in my son. What I love most of all is that Joe is not only training Remy on a physical level for baseball but on a mental level as well.

I believe that I also benefit from Joe because he's shown us all that if you focus on your goals they all can be reached as long as you put in the hard work. Also Remy's teammates benefit because they see the results in his performance and now they want to be on the same level. We travel all the way from Brooklyn, New York to train with Joe in New Jersey because the training and results are that amazing.

Everyday that Remy finishes a training session he has a big smile on his face. That smile comes from all the positive that Joe instills in his workouts. I thank Joe because he not only is helping Remy now but for his whole life ahead.

— Ruben Vazquez from Brooklyn, NY

"...Signing my son up at GameChanger Gym has turned out to be one of the best decisions I have ever made..."

My son Anthony has been going to GameChanger two times a week for the last three months. During this short period of time I have noticed a tremendous difference in him. Not only has he gotten stronger but also he now has more self-confidence and has matured greatly. Anthony is always excited to go GameChanger and usually talks about it all week. This is why recently I have signed Anthony up to start going three times a week. Signing my son up at GameChanger Gym has turned out to be one of the best decisions I have ever made.

During a summer baseball camp Anthony's fastball was clocked at 63mph. After only three short months of working with Joe and his staff, his fastball was recently clocked at 70mph. I am anxious to see what his results will be next spring after working with Joe all winter. I would definitely recommend Joe's program to any parent who was thinking of sending their child to him. Joe has a real connection with all his athletes and will not only make them better athletes but better people too. Thanks for everything.

- Sam Santucci from Springfield, NJ

"...During his time there we have seen a great change in Jeremy's commitment level..."

Our son Jeremy started training at GameChanger in June and during his time there we have seen a great change in Jeremy's commitment level. Since training at GameChanger, Jeremy now looks forward to working out each week, and also his eating habits have become much better.

Since training at GameChanger, Jeremy has hit several home runs and was also the catcher on Cranford's 11U State Champion team. Much of his success on the baseball field can be attributed to his training at GameChanger.

– Jim Ruka from Cranford, NJ

Are you interested in training at GameChanger?
Call us directly at (908) 376-9002 to get
your free, no obligation, assessment for your son.

Or email me at Joe@GameChangerGym.com
for more information on how
we can help your son.

"...As a freshman in high school he is playing on the varsity team..."

My son Jeremy was 13 when he started training with Joe. When Jeremy first started training with Joe, he was very skinny, but over the past 18 months, he has managed to put on 50lbs of lean muscle and his performance on the baseball field has been better then ever before. As a freshman in high school he is playing on the varsity team!
We knew this was the right decision after 1 week of training because every week his body has been changing. While I thought Jeremy was going to get results training with Joe, I had no idea it would be so fast and so incredible.

What I love the most about the training is that it keeps Jeremy busy and healthy. The biggest difference I seen in Jeremy is that he has gained a lot of muscle and he is in the best baseball shape he could be in. It if wasn't for the motivation and confidence Joe gives him, these results would not be possible.

I would recommend Joe's program to parents who want the best possible training for their son. Don't think about it twice because you will see results right away and be fascinated with them.

– Dennis Torres from Brooklyn, New York

Made in the USA
Middletown, DE
19 November 2014